TRAMS IN TROU

BRIAN HINCHLIFFE

1990
PENNINE PUBLICATIONS LTD
SHEFFIELD
in association with
BOND PUBLICATIONS
DONCASTER

First Published November 1990

© Pennine Publications Ltd, 1990

ISBN 0 946055 07 6

Cover Photograph: STALYBRIDGE. 2 April 1908. S.H.M.&D.
Electric Tramway's single-decker No. 29 ran out of control before becoming
derailed at Millbrook. It then ploughed through a wall and fell into the river.

**Printed in Great Britain
by
The KPC Group, London and Ashford, Kent**

INTRODUCTION

It is a saddening thought for today's tram enthusiasts and, indeed, to a great many more to whom the tram seemed a permanent feature of their everyday lives, that there is scarcely anyone below the age of 45 who can even remember the days when the tram was an inevitable sight on the streets of every city and large town in Britain.

Clanking along, or shrieking and whining their way round curves of incredibly small radius, they evoked in most people who knew them the same sort of amused, tolerant affection that one feels for a good-natured carthorse. Indeed, with their lumbering gait, and almost unlimited capacity for hard work, not to mention the sense of oneness that many drivers felt for their charges, there was a striking similarity between trams and carthorses, and both succumbed to advancing technology at much the same time.

The electric tram started to appear on our urban streets in the final years of the last century. This was a time when Councils all over Britain were falling over themselves – especially if they could thereby go one better than their neighbour – to erect ever more grandiose public buildings, and provide ever better services for the local inhabitants. Not least of the latter was public transport and, the cable trams of Edinburgh and London notwithstanding, this almost automatically meant electric trams. Unfortunately, the expense of laying the track and creating an electric supply system, but even more the high cost of maintenance, proved to be far greater, compared with the actual revenue generated, than the sponsors had anticipated in their first flush of enthusiasm.

The sad truth was that the tram was really only appropriate where very large numbers of people had to be moved, day in, day out, within comparatively small areas. Thus, a compact system, such as Sheffield's, carrying some 200,000,000 and more passengers a year, was highly profitable, even allowing for maintaining its track and vehicles in splendid condition, while smaller systems, carrying far fewer passengers, yet with lines meandering miles out into the sparsely populated environs, such as Halifax and Huddersfield, to name only two out of dozens of similarly afflicted undertakings, were always struggling to earn sufficient revenue to cover their operating costs and maintain and renew their capital assets.

This is a book about accidents, but it should not be thought that the tram was a particularly accident-prone vehicle. On the contrary, many tramway systems had superb safety records. To take one example, not a single passenger of the several billion carried ever received a fatal injury whilst on board a Sheffield Corporation tram, during the 60-odd years they ran. Unfortunately, several attributes of the tram could predispose it to certain types of misfortune. In the early days the braking systems on many trams were not as effective and reliable as they later became, and it has to be admitted that many of the early drivers were not as competent in handling the brakes as they should have been. Secondly, the combination of very short radius curves at corners, junctions, and passing loops on single lines, meant that if a driver approached one at too high a speed, derailment was almost inevitable and, because of the tram's comparatively narrow gauge, and usually short wheelbase, derailment was often followed by overturning. It was this, plus the fact that many of the early trams were open-top double-deckers that accounted for a high proportion of the fatal accidents to passengers on British trams over the years. In terms of fatalities, there were only nine accidents in British tramway history when four or more passengers were killed and seven of them involved open-top double-deckers.

The other point one has to record is the frequency with which fog was the initial trigger which set disaster in motion. Not a year goes by without us reading of some multiple pile-up on the motorway when a succession of drivers has driven uncaringly at very high speed into an opaque wall of white mist, to find – if they lived to tell the tale – that the swirling eddies had completely hidden a mêlée of crashed vehicles. Years ago, not a winter ever passed without its quota of days when whole areas disappeared under a layer of thick, grey-green, sulphurous smelling fog, and it came as a surprise even to the present author to discover in how many tram accidents fog played a significant part; not just trams colliding head-on on sections of single track, but drivers approaching bends too fast because they had completely misjudged their location through inability to see any of the usual landmarks. Nor was fog a purely winter phenomenon. Collisions occurred in thick fog in mid-April and early September in Thornaby-on-Tees and Nottingham respectively, while two Rotherham trams met head-on in thick fog during July!

But, it may be said, if the local trams evoked such affection, why devote an entire book to pictures of them at their worst moments, when they were, so to speak, temporarily down on the canvas? The only excuse this author can offer is that accidents have always exercised a peculiar fascination for most human beings. Whether it be firemen struggling to contain a blaze, ambulance men trying desperately to rescue injured victims in a traffic pile-up, or bodies from a crashed aircraft, a railway breakdown gang re-railing stock after a crash, or just relatives standing round a minehead, or shipping office, after news of a calamity, be sure there will be crowds of otherwise uninvolved onlookers ringing the scene. It is arguable that many of the people who flock to Grand Prix car or motor cycle events, air displays, or even a circus high-wire act, are subconsciously hoping that they will have a grandstand view of a disaster. The author firmly believes that if Polaroid cameras had existed in the Stone Age and any photographs had survived, nothing is more certain than that there would be one of a sarsen stone, on its way to Stonehenge, after the leather towing rope had parted, letting it fall off its rollers, and trapping the Druid gaffer in charge of the haulage party!

Problems with the brakes, of one form or another, was undoubtedly the commonest single cause of tram accidents. Basically, at least in later years, trams had three separate and distinct forms of brakes. The simplest and oldest was the wheel brake, consisting of blocks, normally cast iron, brought to bear against the wheel tyres, and actuated by a series of rods connected to a crank handle on the driving platform. A later development was the provision of flat brake blocks which were forced down against the track, and usually called "slipper brakes". When these were first fitted to trams, the blocks were actuated by mechanical linkage from the "big wheel", which was mounted either vertically or horizontally, according to taste, on a column on the driving platform. Usually the wheel brake crank handle and the big wheel were mounted on the same column; in later years the slipper brake was operated either electro-magnetically, or by compressed air, and became that much more powerful in its action, but many smaller systems never adopted this refinement.

Finally, the tram's own motors could be used to provide a powerful braking effect by shutting off power, and making the latent energy of the heavy vehicle turn the commutators, transforming the driving motors effectively into electric generators, feeding current back into the overhead wires.

Individually, each of these systems has possible drawbacks. The handbrake is not powerful enough to bring the tram to a stop rapidly in an emergency and, furthermore, may even lock the wheels solid and cause the tram to skid in certain circumstances, as though it were not being braked at all. A failure in the electric power supply can put the magnetic brake out of action and, if prolonged, might even put the air compressor out of action long enough for the pressure to leak away and put that brake out of action. Finally, the braking effect obtainable from the motors requires the driver to be sufficiently alert, and competent to recognise the situation and make the necessary movement of the power controller instantly.

Accidents involving trams came in many shapes and forms, from being hit by a golf ball, or colliding with a blind man's barrel organ, to catching fire and forming a funeral pyre for some of its passengers; one unfortunate youth was even caught up by the trolley rope and hanged before he could be rescued. For the purpose of this book, however, the author has limited himself to three clearly defined categories: firstly, trams which went over onto their sides; secondly, trams which left the track and collided with walls, or buildings; and thirdly, trams which collided so violently with other trams, or heavy road vehicles, that one or both suffered severe structural damage. For good measure, two air raid victims of the last war have also been included. The geographical coverage has been largely determined by the availability of suitable photographs.

Some systems had more serious accidents than might have been expected from the number of trams they operated, but in their case other factors were usually involved, particularly the very hilly areas in which their trams ran. In their later years Liverpool trams appeared particularly prone to catching fire, while both Glasgow and Liverpool seemed to produce more than the average quota of hell-for-leather drivers – the Kamikaze boys. There was no national speed limit for trams, each route being assessed by the Board of Trade, or Ministry of Transport, Inspecting Officer, who laid down maximum speeds, with special restrictions for more hazardous locations. Trams were, of course, subject to the general maximum speed limit on the road, which was generally 30 miles per hour in built-up areas, but as far as is known, only one driver – in Glasgow, need one add – was ever prosecuted for exceeding the speed limit!

Even when involved in an accident the tram was usually a very safe vehicle to be in. The steel chassis on which the body rested was incredibly strong and could withstand tremendous punishment as will be seen from the picture of the Isle of Thanet tram which went over a 30ft cliff at Margate, and survived to fight another day; likewise the tram in Dewsbury which literally brought the house down (though actually it was an hotel) on top of itself, without collapsing under the weight! Other trams charged through walls, and demolished house sides, with all the panache of a heavy battle tank at full throttle, and almost all of them were subsequently repaired and returned to the fray.

Many of the most vivid memories we retain from childhood involved our presence as onlookers at some scene of catastrophe, carnage, or merely something out of the ordinary humdrum course of events, and this collection of photographs is presented in the hope that it may remind many older readers of some happening they witnessed in their youth. The author would be delighted to borrow, or purchase, good quality photographs of any of the numerous other tram accidents for which there was no room in the present collection; he would, however, respectfully point out that under British and Continental law, copyright in any photograph taken before 1957 only subsists for 50 years from the end of the year in which it was taken.

It only remains to thank the many people who have assisted in the preparation of this book, either with photographs, or information, but particularly Rosie Thacker, Librarian and Archivist at the National Tramway Museum, Crich; J. H. Price, M.C.I.T., Home Editor of "Modern Tramway"; Charles Hall, F.T.I.S., retired Contracts Engineer to South Yorkshire P.T.E.; and J. W. Richmond, whose encyclopaedic knowledge and passion for strict accuracy are a model to all would-be tramway historians. Individual contributions are acknowledged under each photograph.

Brian Hinchliffe,
Sheffield
October 1990

1. BARNSLEY. 2 December 1914. Barnsley & District Electric Traction Company Limited's 4-wheel double-decker No. 4 ran out of control in Eldon Street North and was derailed at the bottom, crashing into the side of a shop, resulting in two people losing their lives and four being injured. *(Courtesy Barnsley Public Library)*

7

2. BATLEY. 16 January 1904. Yorkshire Woollen District Electric Tramways Limited's 4-wheel open-top double-decker No. 55 ran out of control before becoming derailed on the sharp curve from Thorncliffe Road to Track Road, then crashed through the wall of a private garden. Fortunately, nobody was killed but three people were injured.
(Courtesy Norman Ellis Collection)

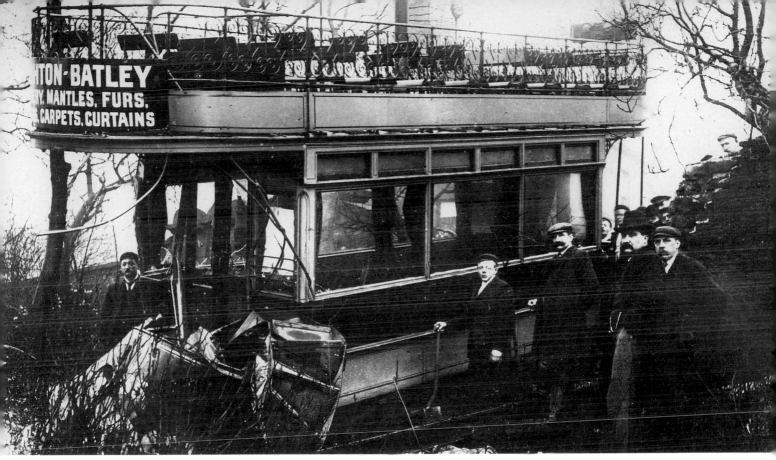

3. BATLEY. 16 January 1904. Another view of the accident on the facing page.

(Courtesy Norman Ellis Collection)

4. BATLEY. 29 August 1904. Yorkshire Woollen District's No. 55 seemed to have a perverse streak. Less than eight months after the accident shown on the previous two pages the driver lost control and it collided with a baker's van in Clerk Green, Batley, becoming derailed in the process, but no-one was injured.

(Courtesy Norman Ellis Collection)

5. BIRMINGHAM. 1 October 1907. For a large operator Birmingham Corporation Tramways had quite a good accident record, but when 4-wheel open-top double-decker No. 22 ran out of control and overturned on the sharp curve at the bottom of Warstone Lane, Brookfields, two people died and twelve were injured. *(Author's Collection)*

6. BIRMINGHAM. 26 June 1916. South Staffordshire Tramway's 4-wheel double-decker No. 46 was derailed while running along Birmingham Corporation track and turned over outside Soho Road Station. Fortunately, nobody was killed, but five were injured. *(Courtesy Norman Ellis Collection)*

7. BOURNEMOUTH. 1 May 1908. One of the worst accidents on a British tramway occurred when Bournemouth's open-top bogie double-decker No. 72 ran out of control on Poole Hill and was derailed at Fairy Glen curve, plunging into the Glen. Seven passengers lost their lives and twenty-six were injured.

(Courtesy Norman Ellis Collection)

8.   BRADFORD.   31 July 1907.   As Bradford Corporation 4-wheel double-decker No. 210 rounded the curve into Barker End Road, the leading axle fractured, making the brakes useless. The car gathered speed before becoming derailed in Church Bank, hitting a warehouse wall and overturning. As a result two people were killed and sixteen injured.

(Courtesy Norman Ellis Collection)

9. BRADFORD. 1 February 1918. There are very few pictures of trams being returned to their proper milieu after overturning, but this photograph of Bradford's 4-wheel double-decker No. 88, which came to grief on the bend in Chapel Lane, Allerton, shows clearly how trams were restored to the vertical. Although there was little apparent damage to the tram, one person was killed and nineteen injured when it turned over.

(Courtesy National Tramway Museum, Crich)

10. BRADLEY, Nr. HUDDERSFIELD.   22 April 1905.   Huddersfield Corporation's bogie double-decker No. 24 ran out of control down the hill at Bradley, before becoming derailed and plunging through a wall, into a copse.   *(Courtesy Norman Ellis Collection)*

11. BURNLEY. 21 December 1923. Burnley Corporation's 4-wheel double-decker No. 10 was one of the very small number of trams which were involved in more than one accident. On this occasion a lorry skidded in the snow and hit the tram which ran backwards and hit houses at Lane Head. Two people were killed and seven injured.

(Courtesy Lancashire Library, Burnley District)

12. BURTON-UPON-TRENT.   8 October 1919.   The Burton & Ashby Light Railway was owned by the Midland Railway Company and was one of the few truly rural tramways in Britain. It had a fleet of 4-wheel open-top double-deckers and one of these, No. 19, started skidding while climbing Bearwood Hill Road, then ran backwards overturning on the curve at the bottom. The conductress and a passenger were killed and sixteen others injured.   *(Courtesy National Tramway Museum, Crich, R. B. Paar Collection)*

13. DEVONPORT. 27 November 1914. Devonport & District Tramways Company had a comparatively short existence, being taken over by Plymouth Corporation Tramways. Not long before that happened its 4-wheel open-top double-decker No. 25 took the turn from Stuart Road into Paradise Road too fast, was derailed and overturned after hitting the wall of the London & South Western Railway Station. Three people were killed and thirty-three injured. *(Courtesy National Tramway Museum, Crich, R. B. Paar Collection)*

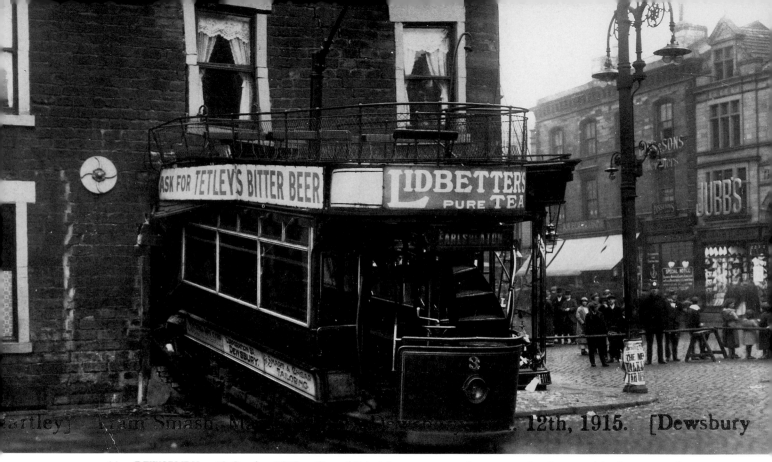

14. DEWSBURY.   12 October 1915.   One of Britain's most spectacular tram crashes happened in the centre of Dewsbury when Dewsbury & Ossett Tramway's 4-wheel open-top double-decker No. 3 ran out of control down Wakefield Road and embedded itself in the front of Hilton's Boot Shop.   *(Courtesy Norman Ellis Collection)*

15. DEWSBURY. 12 October 1915. Shortly after the photograph on the opposite page was taken two floors of the Scarbro Hotel, above the Boot Shop, collapsed onto the tram. Amazingly nobody was killed, but six were injured; the tram suffered surprisingly little damage.

(Courtesy Norman Ellis Collection)

16. DOVER. 19 August 1917. Dover Corporation Tramways was not a very large system, but it had the melancholy distinction of experiencing the worst tram accident seen in Britain. Its 4-wheel open-top double-decker No. 20 was fully loaded with people going to work when it ran out of control and overturned on the curve in Crabble Road. Eleven people were killed and fifty-nine injured. *(Courtesy National Tramway Museum, Crich)*

17.   DOVER.   19 August 1917.   Another view of the same disaster.   *(Courtesy National Tramway Museum, Crich)*

18. EAST WEMYSS.   25 May 1926.   Wemyss & District Tramway's 4-wheel single-decker No. 8 was running back to the depot late at night when it left the track and was only prevented from plunging down a 60ft gorge by a group of trees. There were no casualties.

(Courtesy Kirkcaldy District Library)

19. EDINBURGH, 6 April 1936. Traction engines are fairly substantial monsters, but when this one collided head-on with Edinburgh Corporation's 4-wheel double-decker No. 206 it came off much the worse. Fortunately, nobody was killed, but several of the tram's passengers were cut by broken glass. *(Courtesy D. L. G. Hunter Collection)*

20. EDINBURGH. 8 September 1945. Another Edinburgh tram – 4-wheel double-decker No. 21 – paid an unscheduled call on the Archbishop of St Andrews & Edinburgh, when it was derailed at the bottom of Church Hill and burst through a wall, finishing upright in the Archbishop's garden. Fortunately, there were no casualties.

(Courtesy D. L. G. Hunter Collection)

21. **EXETER.** 7 March 1917. Exeter Corporation Tramway's 4-wheel open-top double-decker No. 17 ran out of control down Fore Street before overturning on Exe Bridge. Unfortunately, one young lady was killed and three other people injured.

(Courtesy Norman Ellis Collection)

22. GATESHEAD. 5 February 1916. Gateshead's 4-wheel single-decker No. 7 ran out of control down Bensham Road, becoming derailed at the sharp bend into Saltwell Road, and overturning onto waste ground. By a cruel coincidence four pedestrians were walking past at the time and could not get out of its way quickly enough, being crushed to death; ten passengers were injured. *(Courtesy Gateshead Public Libraries)*

23. GATESHEAD. 5 February 1916. Another view of the same crash.   (*Courtesy Gateshead Public Libraries*)

Tram Smash, Hx., July 1st, 1906.

24. HALIFAX. 1 July 1906. Halifax Corporation's 4-wheel open-top double-decker No. 94 ran out of control down New Bank, before overturning on North Bridge, resulting in two people being killed and eleven injured.

(Courtesy Norman Ellis Collection)

25. HALIFAX. 22 May 1915. Halifax Corporation's 4-wheel double-decker No. 89 ran out of control and overturned near the bottom of Lee Bank. Fortunately, nobody was killed, but six passengers were injured.

(Courtesy National Tramway Museum, Crich)

26. HUDDERSFIELD. 9 June 1905. Huddersfield's 4-wheel open-top double-decker No. 67 ran away after brake failure on the Edgerton Circular route, then left the track and ploughed through a garden wall. One person was killed but nobody was injured.

(Courtesy Norman Ellis Collection)

27. LANCASTER.   4 March 1912.   A Lancaster Corporation 4-wheel double-decker (Number unknown), ran out of control while descending South Road. After hitting a coal cart the tram eventually left the road at the corner of Thurnham Street and Brock Street. It then hit a bread cart and finished up standing on the pavement in Dalton Square. Nobody was killed, but three people were injured.   *(Courtesy Lancaster Public Library)*

28. LIVERPOOL. 22 January 1906. Liverpool Corporation's 4-wheel double-decker No. 447 ran out of control in Leece Street and was derailed on the curve leading into Renshaw Street, before turning over. Nobody was killed, but eighteen were injured.

(Courtesy Normal Ellis Collection)

79 LONDON, ARCHWAY. 23 June 1906. Metropolitan Electric Tramway's open-top bogie double-decker No. 115 ran out of control on Archway Road, hitting successively a hearse, a furniture van, a motor omnibus, and a cab, before finally hitting another tram. Three people were killed and twenty injured. *(Courtesy Lens of Sutton)*

30. LONDON, CRICKLEWOOD. 27 June 1916. Metropolitan Electric Tramway's open-top double-decker No. 107 was hit by an army lorry in Cricklewood Broadway and overturned as a result. Nobody was killed, but fifteen people were injured.

(Courtesy Lens of Sutton)

31. LONDON, LEE GREEN. 12 June 1914. London County Council Tramway's 4-wheel double-decker No. 150 was derailed at Lee Green and finished up in the entrance to Lee Green Picture Palace. There were no casualties.

(Courtesy Lens of Sutton)

32. LONDON, LEWISHAM.   2 September 1911.   London County Council Tramway's 4-wheel double-decker No. 110 was derailed and overturned on the curve leading from Shardeloes Road into Lewisham High Road. One person was killed and thirty-five injured.   *(Courtesy Lens of Sutton)*

33. LYTHAM ST ANNES. Date unknown. This photograph is believed to show the result of a collision between a Lytham Corporation 4-wheel open-top double-decker and a "Black Maria" near Lytham Police Station, but it has proved impossible to discover any further details.
(Courtesy Norman Ellis Collection)

34. NEWCASTLE-UNDER-LYME. 6 September 1922. An electrical explosion on the driving platform of Potteries Electric Traction's 4-wheel single-decker No. 43 caused the driver to fall into the roadway, whereupon the tram ran out of control. It left the rails and hit two motor vehicles before overturning on a curve in Shelton New Road. Nobody was killed, but eighteen people were injured. *(Courtesy Newcastle-Under-Lyme Public Library)*

35. NEWCASTLE-UPON-TYNE.   26 June 1924.   Newcastle Corporation Tramway's double-decker No. 251 was returning to the depot late at night when it became derailed and crashed into the wall of a house in Stanhope Street. Remarkably there were no serious casualties.   *(Courtesy Newcastle City Libraries)*

36. NEWCASTLE-UPON-TYNE. 18 October 1913. A Tyneside Tramways and Tramroads Company bogie double-decker No. 23 collided late at night in dense fog with 4-wheel trolley wagon No. 27, near Benton Farm. Two company employees were killed and six people injured. *(Courtesy National Tramway Museum, Crich)*

37. PONTYPRIDD.   3 May 1919.   Pontypridd U.D.C. Tramway's open-top bogie double-decker No. 7 left the rails on the very sharp curve leading into Taff Street and ran into the front of Wm Harris's shop, fortunately without any casualties.

(Courtesy Pontypridd Public Library)

38. PONTYPRIDD. 22 March 1920. Pontypridd's double-decker No. 16 ran out of control and became derailed at the corner of Market Street, ending up on the pavement, leaning drunkenly against a building. Fortunately, there were no casualties.

(Courtesy Pontypridd Public Library)

39. QUEENSBURY. 3 December 1920. Two 4-wheel double-decker Halifax trams, Nos. 98 and 50, were blown over at Catherine Slack, Queensbury, during an exceptionally severe gale. As a result the Ministry of Transport Accident Inspector laid down that when the wind exceeded a certain velocity all trams on the Queensbury route were to run with their top deck windows wide open. This decree proved very unpopular with passengers!

(*Courtesy National Tramway Museum, Crich*)

40. RAMSGATE. 26 May 1905. An Isle of Thanet Electric Supply Company Limited's 4-wheel open-top double-deck, No. 47, ran out of control on the Plains of Waterloo, Ramsgate, left the track and embedded itself in a shop front.

(Courtesy Norman Ellis Collection)

41. RAMSGATE. 26 May 1905. Workmen were soon on the scene of the accident on the facing page to shore up the walls of the damaged building. Despite the damage to the tram nobody was killed, but seven were injured.

(Courtesy Norman Ellis Collection)

42. RAMSGATE. 3 August 1905. Isle of Thanet's 4-wheel open-top double-decker No. 41 ran out of control in Madeira Walk, Ramsgate before becoming derailed and plunging 30ft over a cliff. Incredibly nobody was killed and only one person was injured. The tram was subsequently repaired and returned to service.

(Courtesy Norman Ellis Collection)

43. ROCHDALE. 14 February 1914. Rochdale Corporation Tramway's bogie single-decker No. 63 ran out of control in John Street and was derailed on the curve leading into Smith Street. It then ran into a house wall. Nobody was killed, but sixteen were injured. *(Courtesy Rochdale Public Library)*

44. SCARBOROUGH.   16 September 1925.   Scarborough Tramways Company had a good accident record, but it was somewhat marred when 4-wheel double-decker No. 21 skidded on greasy rails then ran backwards down Vernon Road, becoming derailed on the bend and crashing through the roof of Scarborough Aquarium.

(Courtesy Norman Ellis Collection)

45. SCARBOROUGH. 16 September 1925. Another view showing the tram, minus its roof, actually in the Aquarium. No-one was killed in this accident, but two passengers and the driver were injured and history does not record how many fish met an untimely end. *(Courtesy Norman Ellis Collection)*

51

46. SHEFFIELD. 27 March 1902. The earliest accident we are able to show involved Sheffield Corporation's 4-wheel single-decker No. 156. While the driver had left the car to get hot water to mash tea at the Cemetery Gates terminus, the car set off on its own, gaining speed down the hill, until it became derailed at the top of Granville Road. Although at one time it was intended to lay tracks down Granville Road this was never done. As can be seen in the foreground the track terminated abruptly a short distance after the points. The lines of the City Road route can just be discerned behind the legs of the man wearing a peaked cap. *(Courtesy Charles C. Hall Collection)*

47. SOWERBY BRIDGE. 15 October 1907. Halifax Corporation Tramway's 4-wheel open-top double-decker No. 64 was involved in one of the worst British tram crashes. It lost adhesion and started to run backwards in Pye Nest Road, before leaving the rails on the curve at Bolton Brow. After hitting a wall it overturned, resulting in the deaths of six passengers, while thirty-seven others were injured. *(Courtesy Norman Ellis Collection)*

48. STALYBRIDGE. 5 June 1911. S.H.M. & D. Electric Tramway's 4-wheel open-top double-decker No. 44 ran out of control down Ditchcroft Hill, becoming derailed and turning on its side in front of a public house at Millbrook. One person was killed and thirty-three injured. *(Courtesy Stalybridge Public Library)*

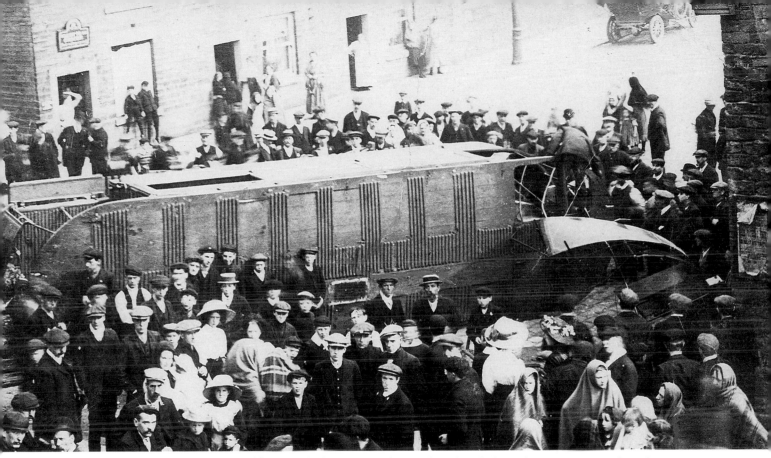

49. STALYBRIDGE. 5 June 1911. A further view of the accident described on the previous page, but after various preliminary measures had been taken for recovering the vehicle. *(Courtesy Stalybridge Public Library)*

50. SUNDERLAND. Exact date unknown, but believed to be 1921 or 1922. Sunderland and District Tramway's 4-wheel double-decker No. 33 had been experiencing brake trouble, and was being driven back to the depot when it ran out of control, left the rails, and overturned.

(*Courtesy National Tramway Museum, Crich*)

51. SWINDON. 1 June 1906. Although Swindon Corporation Tramways had a good safety record, the one accident it did have was a very bad one. Four-wheel open-top double-decker No. 11 ran out of control down Victoria Road and overturned on the curve at the bottom of the hill. As a result five passengers died and thirty were injured. *(Courtesy Norman Ellis Collection)*

52. SWINTON, YORKSHIRE.   30 July 1908.   Mexborough and Swinton Tramways Company's 4-wheel double-decker No. 14 ran out of control through brake failure on Warren Vale Hill, between Rawmarsh and Swinton, before leaving the track and plunging over a wall into a garden. Nobody was killed, but eighteen were injured.

(*Courtesy Norman Ellis Collection*)

53. WALLASEY.   19 March 1907.   Wallasey Corporation Tramway's 4-wheel double-decker No. 56 ran out of control in Seabank Road before leaving the track and finishing on the pavement alongside a garden wall. There were no casualties.

(Courtesy Norman Ellis Collection)

54. WALLINGTON. 1 April 1907. South Metropolitan Electric Tramway's 4-wheel open-top double-decker No. 19 was fully laden and in the hands of a somewhat inexperienced driver who was partially blamed for the tram running away. It overturned on the curve between Park Lane and Ruskin Road, Wallington. Two passengers were killed and thirty-six were injured.

(Courtesy Lens of Sutton)

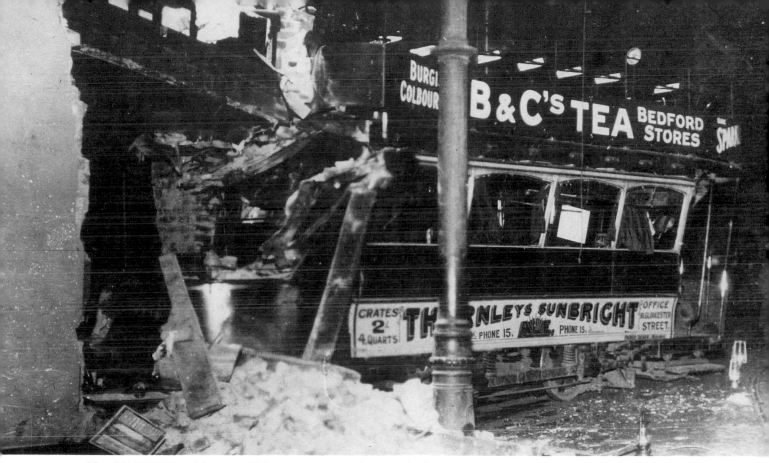

55. WARWICK. 4 January 1916. Leamington and Warwick Electrical Company Limited's 4-wheel open-top double-decker No. 7 ran into the side of the Castle Arms Inn, at Eastgate Arch, Warwick after the driver had left the tram without the handbrake screwed on. Fortunately, nobody was killed, but three people were injured.

(Courtesy Warwick County Record Office)

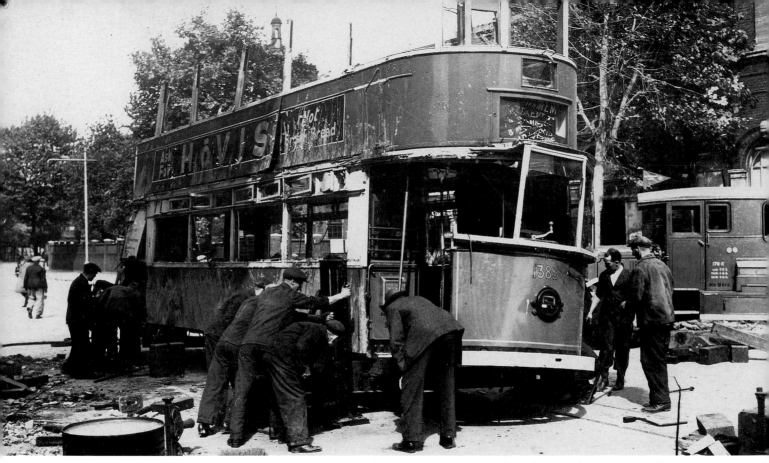

56.   LONDON.   Many trams were damaged, or destroyed, during the London Blitz. London Transport's bogie double-decker No. 1385 suffered extensive damage from bomb blast, but the location is not known.

(Courtesy Lens of Sutton)

57. LONDON. Three more London trams which were damaged during an air raid. Again, the location is not known, but the bogie double-decker in the foreground, whose number appears to end with "00" must surely have been a write-off.

(Courtesy Lens of Sutton)

CHRONOLOGICAL INDEX